As Expounded by Dada Bhagwan

Who Am I?

Originally Compiled in Gujarati by:

Dr. Niruben Amin

Publisher	: **Mr. Ajit C. Patel** **Dada Bhagwan Vignan Foundation** 1, Varun Apartment, 37, Shrimali Society, Opp. Navrangpura Police Station, Navrangpura, Ahmedabad: 380009. Gujarat, India. **Tel.** : +91 79 35002100, +91 9328661166-77
©	**Dada Bhagwan Foundation** 5, Mamta Park Society, B\h. Navgujarat College, Usmanpura, Ahmedabad - 380014, Gujarat, India. Email: info@dadabhagwan.org Tel.: +91 9328661166-77 All Rights Reserved. No part of this publication may be shared, copied, translated or reproduced in any form (including electronic storage or audio recording) without written permission from the holder of the copyright. This publication is licensed for your personal use only.

1st Edition	: 5,000 copies,	January 1994
2nd to **15th Edition**	: 41500 copies,	January 1997 to August 2021
16th Edition	: 5000 copies,	December 2022

Price	: Ultimate humility and the intent that 'I do not know anything'! **Rs. 30.00**
Printer	: **Amba Multiprint** B - 99, Electronics GIDC, K-6 Road, Sector - 25, Gandhinagar-382044. Gujarat, India. Tel. : +91 79 35002142, +91 9328660055

ISBN/eISBN : 978-93-86289-25-4

Printed in India

Trimantra
The Three Mantras That Destroy All Obstacles in Life

Namo Vitaraagaya
I bow to the Ones who are absolutely free from all attachment and abhorrence

Namo Arihantanam
I bow to the living Ones who have annihilated all internal enemies of anger, pride, deceit and greed

Namo Siddhanam
I bow to the Ones who have attained the state of total and final liberation

Namo Aayariyanam
I bow to the Self-realized masters who impart the Knowledge of the Self to others

Namo Uvazzayanam
I bow to the Ones who have received the Knowledge of the Self and are helping others attain the same

Namo Loye Savva Sahunam
I bow to the Ones, wherever they may be, who have received the Knowledge of the Self

Eso Pancha Namukkaro
These five salutations

Savva Pavappanasano
Destroy all demerit karma

Mangalanam Cha Savvesim
Of all that is auspicious

Padhamam Havai Mangalam ‖1‖
This is the highest

Om Namo Bhagavate Vasudevaya ‖2‖
I bow to the Ones who have attained the absolute Self in human form

Om Namah Shivaya ‖3‖
I bow to all human beings who have become instruments for the salvation of the world

Jai Sat Chit Anand
Awareness of the Eternal is Bliss

Books of Akram Vignan of Dada Bhagwan

1. Adjust Everywhere
2. Anger
3. Aptavani - 1
4. Aptavani - 2
5. Aptavani - 4
6. Aptavani - 5
7. Aptavani - 6
8. Aptavani - 8
9. Aptavani - 9
10. Autobiography of Gnani Purush A.M.Patel
11. Avoid Clashes
12. Brahmacharya: Celibacy Attained With Understanding
13. Death: Before, During and After...
14. Flawless Vision
15. Generation Gap
16. Harmony in Marriage
17. Life Without Conflict
18. Money
19. Noble Use of Money
20. Non-Violence
21. Pratikraman: The Master Key That Resolves All Conflicts (Abridged & Big Volume)
22. Pure Love
23. Right Understanding to Help Others
24. Science of Karma
25. Science of Speech
26. The Current Living Tirthankara Shree Simandhar Swami
27. Simple and Effective Science for Self-Realization
28. The Essence of All Religion
29. The Fault Is of the Sufferer
30. The Guru and the Disciple
31. The Hidden Meaning of Truth and Untruth
32. The Practice of Humanity
33. Trimantra
34. Whatever Has Happened Is Justice
35. Who Am I?
36. Worries

'Dadavani' Magazine is published every month in English

Who Is Dada Bhagwan?

In June 1958, around 6 o'clock one evening, amidst the hustle and bustle of the Surat railway station while seated on a bench, 'Dada Bhagwan' manifested completely within the sacred bodily form of Ambalal Muljibhai Patel. Nature revealed a remarkable phenomenon of spirituality! In the span of an hour, the vision of the universe was unveiled to him! Complete clarity for all spiritual questions such as, 'Who are we? Who is God? Who runs the world? What is karma? What is liberation?' etc. was attained.

What He attained that evening, He imparted to others through his original Scientific experiment (*Gnan Vidhi*) in just two hours! This has been referred to as the *Akram* path. *Kram* means to climb up sequentially, step-by-step while *Akram* means step-less, a shortcut, the elevator path!

He, himself, would explain to others who Dada Bhagwan is by saying, "The one visible before you is not Dada Bhagwan. I am the *Gnani Purush* and the One who has manifested within is Dada Bhagwan who is the Lord of the fourteen worlds. He is also within you, and within everyone else too. He resides unmanifest within you, whereas here [within A. M. Patel], He has manifested completely! I, myself, am not God (*Bhagwan*); I also bow down to the Dada Bhagwan who has manifest within me."

❖ ❖ ❖ ❖ ❖

The Current Link to Attain Self-Realization

After attaining the Knowledge of the Self in 1958, absolutely revered Dada Bhagwan (Dadashri) traveled nationally and internationally to impart spiritual discourse and Self-realization to spiritual seekers.

During his lifetime itself, Dadashri had given the spiritual power to Pujya Dr. Niruben Amin (Niruma) to bestow Self-realization to others. In the same way, after Dadashri left his mortal body, Pujya Niruma conducted spiritual discourses (*satsang*) and imparted Self-realization to spiritual seekers, as an instrumental doer. Dadashri had also given Pujya Deepakbhai Desai the spiritual power to conduct *satsang*. At present, with the blessings of Pujya Niruma, Pujya Deepakbhai travels nationally and internationally to impart Self-realization as an instrumental doer.

After Self-realization, thousands of spiritual seekers prevail in a state free from bondage and dwell in the experience of the Self, whilst carrying out all their worldly responsibilities.

❖ ❖ ❖ ❖ ❖

Note About This Translation

The *Gnani Purush*, Ambalal M. Patel, also commonly known as 'Dadashri' or 'Dada', gave spiritual discourses that were in the form of answers to questions asked by spiritual aspirants. These discourses were recorded and compiled into books by Pujya Dr. Niruben Amin in the Gujarati language.

Dadashri had said that it would be impossible to translate His *satsangs* and the Knowledge about the Science of Self-realization word for word into other languages, because some of the meaning would be lost in the process. Therefore, in order to understand precisely the *Akram* Science of Self-realization, He stressed the importance of learning Gujarati.

However, Dadashri did grant His blessings to translate His words into other languages so that spiritual seekers could benefit to a certain degree and later progress through their own efforts. This book is not a literal translation, but great care has been taken to preserve the essence of His original message.

Spiritual discourses have been and continue to be translated from Gujarati. For certain Gujarati words, several translated words or even sentences are needed to convey the meaning, hence many Gujarati words have been retained within the translated text for better understanding. Where the Gujarati word is used for the first time, it is italicized, followed by a translation explaining its meaning in parenthesis. Subsequently, only the Gujarati word is used in the text that follows. This serves a two-fold benefit; firstly, ease of translation and reading, and secondly, make the reader more familiar with the Gujarati words, which is critical for a deeper understanding of this spiritual Science. The content in square brackets provides further clarity regarding the matter, which is not present in the original Gujarati content.

This is a humble attempt to present to the world, the essence of His Knowledge. While reading this translation, if there is any contradiction or discrepancy, then it is the mistake of the translators and the understanding of the matter should be clarified with the living *Gnani* to avoid misinterpretation.

❖ ❖ ❖ ❖ ❖

Special Note to the Reader

The Self is the Soul (*Atma*) within all living beings.

The term pure Soul is used by the *Gnani Purush* for the awakened Self, after the *Gnan Vidhi*. The word Self, with an uppercase 'S', refers to the awakened Self which is separate from the worldly-interacting self, which is written with a lowercase 's'.

Wherever Dadashri uses the term 'we', 'us', or 'our', He is referring to Himself, the *Gnani Purush*.

Similarly, the use of You or Your in the middle of a sentence, with an uppercase first letter, or 'You', 'Your' in single quotes at the beginning of the sentence, refers to the state of the awakened Self or *Pragnya*. This is an important distinction for the correct understanding of the difference between the awakened Self and the worldly-interacting self.

Wherever the name 'Chandubhai' is used, the reader should substitute his or her name and read the matter accordingly.

The masculine third person pronoun 'he' and likewise the object pronoun 'him' have been used for the most part throughout the translation. Needless to say, 'he' includes 'she' and 'him' includes 'her'.

For reference, a glossary of all the Gujarati words is either provided at the back of this book or available on our website at:

http://www.dadabhagwan.org/books-media/glossary/

❖ ❖ ❖ ❖ ❖

Editorial

A person does not accept anything that he comes across in life, without fully realizing [experiencing] it. Everything has been realized, it is only the Self that has not been realized! Since infinite lives, only the realization of 'who am I?' has been hampered, and that is indeed why this wandering is not coming to an end! How can this realization happen?

It is only the One who has realized the Self who can easily make others realize It! This manifestation of the magnificence, splendor, energies, and glory of the absolute Self in the human body is none other than the *Gnani* (the One with Knowledge of the Self) Himself! The *Gnani Purush* is the One who has nothing left to be Known or to be done in this world! Such a *Gnani Purush*, the absolutely revered Dadashri, is present amongst us in this era of the time cycle, and using our own language, a simple, vernacular language that we all understand, He easily solves the fundamental question of 'who am I?' which everyone has.

It is not limited to just that. [Questions such as,] 'What is this world? How does it function? Who is the doer? What is God? What is liberation (*moksha*)? Who can be considered to be a *Gnani Purush*? Who is Lord Simandhar Swami? What is the difference between saints, gurus, and the *Gnani Purush*? How can the *Gnani* be recognized? What can the *Gnani* do? Moreover, what is Dadashri's *Akram* path?' [are also solved.] Since infinite lives, one has progressed on the path to liberation step-by-step, but can't there also be a 'lift' [elevator] on the path to liberation? Through the *Akram* path, there is liberation even whilst living a worldly life. And how can liberation be attained? Dada gives the complete understanding of all this and leads us to adopt the right direction.

What is the experience after the realization of 'who am

I'? Despite continuing to settle worldly life, one can remain in the experience of the absolutely unaffected state as the Self. Even amidst mental, physical, and externally-induced problems, One can continuously remain in a blissful state, free from the effect of such problems. This is the experience of thousands of *mahatmas* (Self-realized Ones in *Akram Vignan*) after attaining *Akram Vignan* (the spiritual Science of the step-less path to Self-realization)! In order for spiritual aspirants to attain all of this, it is our ardent prayer that this compilation will be like a lighthouse aiding them on the path to liberation.

- Dr. Niruben Amin

❖ ❖ ❖ ❖ ❖

Who Am I?

[1] Who Am I?

The Name and 'You' Are Separate

Dadashri: What is your name?

Questioner: My name is Chandubhai.

Dadashri: Are You really Chandubhai?

Questioner: Yes.

Dadashri: Chandubhai is your name. Isn't Chandubhai your name? Are You Yourself Chandubhai or is your name Chandubhai?

Questioner: That is just a name.

Dadashri: Yes, so who are You? If Chandubhai is your name, then who are You? Are You and your name not separate? If You are separate from your name, then who are You? Do you understand what I am trying to say? If you say, "These are my eyeglasses," then you and the eyeglasses are separate, aren't they? Similarly, do you still not feel that You are separate from your name?

Just as if a shop were to be named 'General Traders', there is no offence in that. However, if we were to say to the shop owner, "Hey General Traders, come here!" then the shop owner would respond, "My name is actually Jayantilal, and General Traders is the name of my shop." So the name of the shop owner is separate, and the shop owner is separate, the merchandise in the shop is separate; everything is separate, isn't it? What do you think?

Questioner: That makes sense.

Dadashri: Whereas here, people insist, "No, I myself am Chandubhai." So here, not only are you the sign on the shop but you are also the owner of the shop! 'Chandubhai' is just a means of identification.

Are You Getting Affected? Then You Are Not Prevailing as the Self!

Yes, it is not that you are not Chandubhai entirely. You are Chandubhai, but 'you are Chandubhai' is correct by the relative viewpoint.

Questioner: 'I' am actually the Self (*Atma*), but my name is Chandubhai.

Dadashri: Yes, but if someone were to swear at Chandubhai, then does it affect you?

Questioner: I do get affected.

Dadashri: Then you are Chandubhai, you are not [prevailing as] the Self. If You are [prevailing as] the Self, then You would not get affected. And the fact that you are getting affected means that you indeed are Chandubhai.

You are taking on the verbal abuse that is being hurled in the name of Chandubhai. If someone is speaking negatively about Chandubhai [in the next room], then you end up putting your ear to the wall and start listening. If someone were to ask you, "What is the wall saying to you?" Then, you would say, "No, not the wall, behind the wall they are talking about me and that is what I am listening to." Now, who are they really talking about? About Chandubhai. Hey, but You are not Chandubhai. If You are the Self, then You would not accept anything addressed to Chandubhai.

Questioner: In reality, 'I' am indeed the Self, right?

Dadashri: You have not yet become the Self, have you! You are still Chandubhai, aren't you! The belief that 'I am Chandubhai' is a false attribution (*aaropit bhaav*). The belief that 'I indeed am Chandubhai' has set in for you; that is a wrong belief.

[2] Beliefs, Wrong and Right

There Are So Many Wrong Beliefs

This belief of yours, that 'I am Chandubhai,' does not disappear even at night in your sleep, does it! Moreover, people get you married off, and then they say, "You are this woman's husband," so then you accept the role of a husband and act like one. After that, you keep reiterating that 'I am her husband.' Would anyone be a husband forever? If you end up divorcing, then from the very next day, would you be her husband? So, all these wrong beliefs have set in.

Thus, 'I am Chandubhai' is a wrong belief. Then 'I am this woman's husband' is the second wrong belief. 'I am a devotee of Lord Krishna' is the third wrong belief. 'I am a lawyer' is the fourth wrong belief. 'I am this boy's father' is the fifth wrong belief. 'I am this boy's maternal uncle' is the sixth wrong belief. 'I am fair-skinned' is the seventh wrong belief. 'I am forty-five years old' is the eighth wrong belief. 'I am this man's business partner' is also a wrong belief. If you say, "I am an income taxpayer," then that too is a wrong belief. How many such wrong beliefs must have set in?

Change in the Position of the 'I'

This [belief of] 'I am Chandubhai' is egoism (*ahamkaar*). This is because to falsely claim 'I am' when one is in fact not that, that is called egoism.

Questioner: How can there be egoism in saying, "I am Chandubhai"? If someone says, "I am like this, I am like that," that would be a different matter, but if he casually says, "I am Chandubhai," where is the ego in that?

Dadashri: Even if he says it casually, does the ego withdraw? Even if he says, "My name is Chandubhai," casually, it is still egoism indeed. This is because you do not know who You are, and you identify yourself with that which you are not. That is all egoism indeed, isn't it!

[To say] 'You are Chandubhai' is for a 'dramatic' purpose only [for playing your role in worldly interactions]. So there is no problem with saying, "I am Chandubhai," but the belief that 'I am Chandubhai' should not set in.

Questioner: Yes, otherwise the state of the 'I' will have taken hold [in the wrong place].

Dadashri: If the 'I' is placed in its right place, then it is not egoism. The 'I' is not in its original place, it is in a wrongly attributed place, hence it is egoism. When the 'I' withdraws from the wrongly attributed place and gets positioned in the right place, then the ego disappears. Therefore, the 'I' is not to be removed, the 'I' is to be positioned in its exact place.

Is One Unknown to One's Own Self?

In fact, for infinite lives, one has attempted to remain hidden from one's own Self. Is it not astonishing that not only has one remained hidden from one's own Self, but one has also known everything that is not of one's Self?

How long will you remain hidden from your own Self? For how long will you remain [this way]? The only purpose of this life is to realize 'who am I'. The purpose of the human life is solely to figure out 'who am I'. Otherwise, until then, you will continue wandering aimlessly. You will have to know 'who am I', won't you? Will you need to know 'who am I' or not?

[3] The Experiment to Separate 'I' and 'My'

Separate 'I' and 'My'

If you were told to separate 'I' and 'my' with a 'separator', then would you actually be able to separate them? Is it worth separating 'I' and 'my' or not? Sooner or later, you will have to know this, won't you! Separate 'I' and 'my'. Just as there is a 'separator' that separates cream from milk, similarly, separate this ['I' and 'my'].

At the moment, are you identifying with 'my'? Are you the 'I' alone, or is the 'my' there alongside?

Questioner: The 'my' is bound to be there alongside, isn't it!

Dadashri: What are all the things that fall under 'my' for you?

Questioner: My house and all the things inside my house.

Dadashri: Are all of those things considered to be Yours [of the Self]? And who does the wife belong to?

Questioner: She is also mine.

Dadashri: And whose children are these?

Questioner: They are also mine.

Dadashri: And whose watch is this?

Questioner: It is also mine.

Dadashri: And whose hands are these?

Questioner: These hands are also mine.

Dadashri: Then you will also say, "My head, my body, my feet, my ears, my eyes." You refer to all these parts of the body as 'mine', but who is it that says 'mine'? Have you never thought about that? You say, "My name is Chandubhai," and later you say, "I am Chandubhai"; do you not feel there is a contradiction in this?

Questioner: Yes, I do.

Dadashri: You are Chandubhai; currently, both 'I' and 'my' are encompassed in that. The two railway lines of 'I' and 'my' are completely separate; they always run parallel, they never merge. Nevertheless, you believe them to be one. Having understood this, separate the 'my'. Set aside everything that falls under 'my'. For example, [you say,] "My heart"; so set that aside. What other things do we need to separate from this body?

Questioner: The feet and all the sensory organs.

Dadashri: Yes, everything. The five sensory organs (*gnanendriya*; the body systems through which the knowledge of sight, hearing, touch, smell, and taste is acquired) and the five organs of action (*karmendriya*; the eliminative organs, genital organs, feet, hands, and tongue).

And then do you say, "My mind" or "I am mind"?

Questioner: I say, "My mind."

Dadashri: Do you not say, "My intellect"?

Questioner: Yes.

Dadashri: And you say, "My *chit* (the subtle component

of vision and knowledge in the inner functioning instrument which is composed of the mind, intellect, *chit*, and ego)," don't you?

Questioner: Yes.

Dadashri: Then do you say, "My egoism," or do you say, "I am egoism"?

Questioner: My egoism.

Dadashri: If you say, "My egoism," then you will be able to maintain separation to that extent. However, you do not know what lies beyond this, what part is Yours. So then complete separation does not happen. You only know what is Yours to a certain extent. You only know the gross parts; you do not know the subtle parts at all. As a matter of fact, the subtle parts need to be deducted, then the subtler parts need to be deducted, then the subtlest parts need to be deducted; that is a task only for the *Gnani Purush*.

However, if you keep on subtracting away each of the spare parts, then it is possible to separate the 'I' and the 'my', isn't it? If you keep on deducting 'my' from 'I', what is it that finally remains? If you set aside the 'my', then what is it that ultimately remains?

Questioner: The 'I'.

Dadashri: So that 'I' is precisely what You are! That is all. That 'I' needs to be realized.

Questioner: So after such a separation, am I to understand that whatever is left over, that is what 'I' am?

Dadashri: Yes, whatever remains after the separation, that is who You are. The 'I' is what You actually are. This will need to be examined, won't it?

So isn't this an easy method, provided the 'I' and 'my' are separated?

Questioner: It does appear to be simple, but that happens only when the subtler and subtlest levels become separate, isn't it? That is not possible without a *Gnani*, is it?

Dadashri: Yes, the *Gnani Purush* will show you that. That is why 'we' say, "Separate 'I' and 'my' with the *Gnani's* separator." What do the writers of the scriptures call this 'separator'? They refer to it as the Knowledge of separation (*bhed Gnan*). How are you going to do the subtraction without the Knowledge of separation? You do not have the Knowledge of separation, the Knowledge of what things are Yours and what things are not Yours. The Knowledge of separation means: All this goes in 'mine' and 'I' am separate from that. Therefore, if you remain in touch with the *Gnani Purush*, then that Knowledge of separation will be attained, and then it will become separate for you.

If the separation between 'I' and 'my' is made, then it is very easy, isn't it? Is spirituality easy or difficult through this method that 'we' have shown? Otherwise, the living beings of this era of the time cycle will keep on reading scriptures to the point of exhaustion.

Questioner: We need someone like you to help us understand, don't we?

Dadashri: Yes, there is that need. However, there are not a lot of *Gnani Purush* who are around, are there! They are rarely around; so get your work done during that time. Take the *Gnani Purush's* 'separator' for an hour or so; there is no charge for that! Get the separation done through that. So then the 'I' becomes separate; otherwise, it would not! Once the 'I' becomes separate, all the work gets done. The essence of all the scriptures is just this much.

If you want to become the Self, then you will have to surrender all that falls under 'my'. If you surrender the 'my' to the *Gnani Purush*, then you will be left with the 'I' alone. 'I' with 'my' is known as the embodied self (*jeevatma*). 'I am, and all of this is mine,' is the state as the embodied self. And 'I am 'I' alone and all of this is not mine,' is the state as the absolute Self (*Parmatma*). Therefore, it is due to the 'my' that liberation (*moksha*) does not happen. If the realization (*bhaan*) of 'who am I' arises, then the 'my' leaves. If the 'my' leaves, then everything leaves.

'My' is the relative department and the 'I' is Real. Meaning, the 'I' is never temporary, the 'I' is permanent. 'My' is temporary. Therefore, you should find the 'I' amidst all this.

[4] Who Is Your Superior in the World?

Only the Gnani Makes You Realize the 'I'

Questioner: This point about Knowing 'who am I'; how is that possible while remaining in worldly life (*sansaar*)?

Dadashri: Then where else can that be Known? Is there any other place besides worldly life where one lives? In fact, everyone in this world leads a worldly life and remains in worldly life. Over here, it is possible to Know 'who am I'. This Science is indeed for the purpose of understanding who You are. Come here, 'we' will make you realize Your true Self.

And in terms of all the questions 'we' ask you, 'we' do not expect you to set out to do it. You do not have the capability to do so. That is why 'we' are telling you that 'we' will do everything for you. So there is no need for you to worry. Actually, you should first Know, 'Who am I truly and what is worth Knowing? What is the truth? What are the correct facts? What is this world? What is all of this? What is the absolute Self (*Parmatma*)?'

Does the absolute Self exist? The absolute Self indeed exists, and It is indeed within you. Why are you searching for It externally? However, it is only when someone opens the 'door' for you that you can See It, isn't it! That 'door' has been shut in such a way that it is impossible to ever open it on your own. That is a task only for the *Gnani Purush*, the One who has Himself become liberated, and thus, can liberate others.

Your Own Mistakes Are Your Superior

God (*Bhagwan*) is actually Your Real form (*Swaroop*). There is no superior who is above You, there is no higher authority above You. There is no one who can do anything at all to You. 'You' are completely independent; you are only bound by your own mistakes.

No one is superior to You, nor can any living being interfere with You. There are innumerable living beings, but no living being can ever interfere with You. And these people who do interfere with you are doing so because of your own mistake. This is the result of the interference that you have done in the past. 'We' are saying this after having Seen it for 'ourselves'.

In the following two statements, 'we' are giving a guarantee, and that is when a person can remain liberated. What 'we' say is this:

"There is no one in the world who is Your superior. Your blunders and your mistakes are your superiors. In the absence of these two, You are indeed the absolute Self."

And furthermore, "No one can interfere in the slightest with You. No living being is in a position whereby it can interfere even in the slightest with another living being; that is how this world is."

These two statements bring about closure and inner satisfaction to everything.

[5] Who Is the Doer in This World?

The Reality of Who Runs This World

All these entanglements have arisen simply because the facts are not known. Now do you want to know what you already know, or do you want to know what you do not know?

'What is this world? How did it come into existence? Who is the creator? What do You have to do with the world? What do You have to do with your relatives? What is the basis for running your business? Am 'I' the doer or is there another doer?' It is necessary to know all of this, isn't it?

Questioner: Yes.

Dadashri: So let us first talk about what needs to be Known. Who do you think has created this world? Who would have made a world with such entanglements? What is your opinion?

Questioner: God definitely must have made it.

Dadashri: So then why is the entire world consumed with worries? There is absolutely no situation that is free of worries.

Questioner: Everyone worries, right?

Dadashri: Yes, but if God had made this world, then why would He have made it full of worries? You should get Him arrested by the CBI [Central Bureau of Investigation]!

However, God is not guilty at all! It is just that these people consider Him to be the culprit.

In reality, God is not the creator of this world at all. This world has simply arisen through scientific circumstantial evidence. So this is all a natural creation. In Gujarati, I refer to this as *vyavasthit shakti* (the energy of scientific circumstantial evidence). This is actually a very subtle fact.

That Cannot Be Considered Liberation at All!

Even a small child says, "God made the world." Even a renowned saint will say, "God made it." This is a worldly viewpoint; it does not go beyond the physical world.

If God were the creator, then He would always be our superior and there would be no such thing as liberation (*moksha*). However, there is such a thing as liberation. God is not the creator. People who understand liberation do not believe God to be the creator. 'Liberation' and 'God as the creator', these two concepts are contradictory. A creator means that He would be considered a benefactor forever, and as a benefactor, He would always remain our superior.

Then Who Made God?

Now, if we were to say that God is the creator in Reality, then a logical person would ask, "Then who made God?" So questions arise. People tell me, "We feel that God runs this world. You say this isn't so, but it is difficult for us to accept this." So I respond by asking, "If I were to accept that God is the doer, then who made God? Tell me this much. And who created this creator [God]?" It is logical that if there is a creator, then there has to be someone who created the creator. However, then there would be no end to this, so this concept is incorrect.

There Is Neither a Beginning nor an End to This World

Thus, [the world] has come about without anybody creating it, nobody has created it. Nobody has created it, so who can we possibly ask about this? I, too, was searching for the one who had created such a chaotic mess and taken on such a liability! I searched everywhere, but I did not find him anywhere.

I told the foreign scientists, "Discuss with me the proof you have of God being the creator. If He is the creator, then tell me, in which year did He create [the world]?" To which they replied, "We don't know the year." I asked them, "But did it have a beginning or not?" They replied, "Yes, there was a beginning." If they claim there is a creator, then of course there has to be a beginning, doesn't there! That which has a beginning inevitably comes to an end. In fact, this world has no end. There is no beginning, so how can there be an end? It is actually without a beginning or an end. That which has no beginning cannot have a creator; don't you think so?

God's Correct Address

Then the foreign scientists asked me, "So does God not exist?" So I told them, "If God did not exist, then no one would experience these feelings of happiness or misery that arise. So God definitely exists." They asked me, "Where does God reside?" I said, "Where do you think He resides?" To which they replied, "Up above." I asked, "Where does He live up above? What is His street number? Do you know which street He lives on? Do you have the correct address in order to mail a letter to Him?" There is no higher authority up there. I have visited all the places. Everyone says that He is up above, they point upwards. So I thought, 'Everyone is saying this, so there has to be something.' So I set out to investigate everywhere up there, but there is nothing but empty space up there, there is nobody up there. Nobody resides up there. So then the foreign scientists asked me, "Could you provide the correct address of God?" I told them, "Write it down. God is in every creature whether visible or invisible, not in [man-made] creation."

This tape recorder is a creation. God does not reside in any man-made things. God is present in all things that exist naturally.

Using the Principles According to One's Own Convenience

So this is scientific circumstantial evidence. It is when so many circumstances come together that work gets done. In that, you keep claiming with egoism, "I did it." In fact, when things turn out well, people claim, "I did it," and when they do not turn out well, they say, "My circumstances are not favorable right now"! Don't our people say such things? Our people believe in circumstances, don't they?

Questioner: Yes.

Dadashri: When one earns money, he indulges in the pleasure that arises from the doership of earning, and when he incurs a loss, he makes excuses. If you ask him, "What's going on, mate? Why have you become like this lately?" Then he replies, "God is angry with me."

Questioner: One ends up using the principles according to his own convenience.

Dadashri: Yes. According to his own convenience, but one should not make such an accusation towards God. It is fine if you accuse a lawyer or if you accuse someone else, but can an accusation be made towards God! A lawyer can file a suit and claim damages, but who will file this suit? The result of this causes terrible bondage in the next life. Can you accuse God?

Questioner: No.

Dadashri: Or else one will say, "My stars are not favorable." Or else one will say, "My business partner is dodgy." He will raise objections with his business partner. Or he will say, "My daughter-in-law is bad luck." However, he will not take on the blame himself! He never admits his own responsibility. I had spoken to a person from outside of India. He asked, "Why don't Indians take on the responsibility for an offence that has been committed?" I replied, "That itself is the Indian puzzle. If there is the biggest puzzle of all, it would be that of the Indian [puzzle]."

Scientific Circumstantial Evidence

So discuss this, discuss anything you want to. Discuss things so that you get all of the clarifications.

Questioner: I did not understand this statement 'scientific circumstantial evidence'.

Dadashri: All of this is based on scientific circumstantial evidence. Not even a single *parmanu* (the smallest, most indivisible and indestructible particle of inanimate matter) in this world can be changed. If you sit down to eat right now, then you yourself do not know what you are going to eat! The person who is going to cook the food does not know what will be on the menu tomorrow! How this ends up happening is also a wonder! How much you will be able to eat and how much you will not be able to eat; all the *parmanu* for that are already arranged [within].

The fact that you have met me today, on what basis did this happen? It is only scientific circumstantial evidence. There are very subtle causes behind this. Figure out what these causes are.

Questioner: But how can we figure them out?

Dadashri: The fact that you have come here right now is not in your hands. You simply believe and have the egoism that 'I came and I went.' You claim, "I came," but I ask, "Why didn't you come yesterday?" So you point to your legs. So what should one take that to mean?

Questioner: That my legs were aching.

Dadashri: Yes, your legs were aching. When you blame your legs, don't you understand whether you brought yourself here or whether your legs brought you here?

Questioner: Well, it would still be considered as 'I have come,' wouldn't it?

Dadashri: It is indeed you who have come, isn't it? If your legs were aching, then would you come again?

Questioner: It was my own desire to come here; that is why I have come.

Dadashri: Yes, you had the desire, so you came. However, it was because your legs and everything else was functioning well that you were able to come here, isn't it? What if they weren't functioning well?

Questioner: Then I would not have been able to come, that is true.

Dadashri: So are you able to come here on your own accord? Just as if a person were to come here in a carriage and claim, "I came, I came." Then I would tell him, "Your legs are paralyzed, so how is it that you've come here?" To which he would reply, "I came in a carriage. But I am the one who came, I am indeed the one who came." "But hey, did you come or did the carriage bring you?" Then he would reply, "The carriage brought me." So I would ask,

"Is it the carriage that brought you or is it the bullocks pulling the carriage who brought you?"

So, this is far from reality! But just imagine, one has believed the wrong things! If all these circumstances are favorable, then one can come here. Otherwise, one cannot.

If you have a headache, then even after arriving here, you would have to go back. If you were the one who came here and went back [on your own accord], then you cannot give the excuse of having a headache, can you? So, was it your head that brought you here or was it you who came here? Or if you come across someone on your way here and he says, "Come Chandubhai, come with me," then you would have to turn back. Thus, if the circumstances are favorable, as long as you don't encounter any obstacles on the way here, that is when you are able to come here.

How Much Power Do You Have?

'You' have never even eaten, have You! It is actually Chandubhai who eats all of this and you believe 'I have eaten.' Chandubhai is the one who eats and Chandubhai is the one who defecates. You are trapped in this for no reason. Do you understand this?

Questioner: Please explain that.

Dadashri: No one has been born in this world who has the independent power to empty his bowels. No one has the independent power to empty his bowels, so what other power does he have? As it is, when a few things go according to one's plans, he believes, 'Everything happens only because of me.' He will know the truth when he becomes constipated!

Once, I had gathered in Vadodara, ten to twelve doctors from other countries. I told them, "You do not have the independent energy to empty your bowels." So they were all taken aback. Then I told them, "You will realize this when you become constipated. In such a situation, you will have to seek help from someone else." Therefore, this is not your independent energy at all. It is through illusion that you have come to believe nature's energy to be your own energy. To believe that which is not under your control as being under your control is called illusion. Did you understand this to a certain extent? Did you understand it a little?

Questioner: Yes, I understand.

Dadashri: Even if you understand this much, the final solution will come about. All these people say, "I did this much penance, I chanted, I fasted"; all of that is an illusion. Nevertheless, the world will always carry on like this. People cannot refrain from expressing the ego. That is one's nature, isn't it?

The Doer, the Evidentiary Doer...

Questioner: If one is not truly the doer, then who is the doer? And what is his real form?

Dadashri: The fact is; one is actually an evidentiary (*naimitik*) doer. One is definitely not an independent doer, but he is an evidentiary doer. So he is a doer as in a parliamentary process. What does a parliamentary process mean? Just as everyone votes in a parliament, and one has to give his own vote and based on that, one makes the decision, "I will definitely have to do this." So he is the doer to this extent, to the extent of the planning that takes place. One himself does the planning. There is doership only in the planning; one gives the endorsement in the planning. However, the world does not know about this. The 'feed' [intent] is the output from the small 'computer' and that 'feed' is then inputted into the big 'computer'.

In this way, the planning that takes place is then fed into the big 'computer'. The big 'computer' then gives off the corresponding effect. So in this lifetime, the entire life is in the form of discharge, the causes for which had been charged in the past life. So this lifetime, from birth to death, is in the form of discharge. Nothing is in one's hands, it is under the authority of another entity. Once the planning has taken place, everything falls under the authority of another entity. That entity then plays a role in bringing forth the effect in concrete existence. So the overt effect is different. The overt effect is subject to the authority of another entity. Do you understand this? This is a very profound point.

Karma Is Bound Through Doership

Questioner: What should I do to become free from the bondage of karma?

Dadashri: These karma are dependent upon the doer. So karma can only be bound if one is the doer. If one is not the doer, then karma is not bound. Why is one the doer? When one becomes fixed on the false attribution of 'I am Chandubhai' (*aaropit bhaav*), he becomes the doer. If One comes into the Self, then He is not the doer at all. When one says, "I did it," he becomes the doer. So he gives support to karma. Now, if he does not become the doer, then the karma shed away; as long as they are not supported, they shed away. So there is [charging of] karma as long as there is a sense of doership.

*"Chhoote dehadhyaas to nahin karta tu karma,
Nahin bhokta tu tehno ej dharma no marma."*

"When the belief that 'I am the body' leaves, then You are not the doer of karma,
Nor are You the sufferer of karma; that is indeed the essence of religion."

- Shrimad Rajchandra

At present, you believe 'I am Chandubhai,' so the Self and the non-Self have become one. However, both of these entities are separate. 'You' are separate and Chandubhai is separate. However, as long as you are not aware of this, what can be done? The *Gnani Purush* separates them through *bhed Vignan* (the Science that separates the Self from the non-Self). So once You become separate, You do not have to 'do' anything, Chandubhai will continue doing everything.

[6] Who Can Impart Bhed Gnan?

The Scientific Separation of the Self and the Non-Self

Suppose both gold and copper are mixed together in this ring. If you take it to your hometown and ask your family members, "Please separate the gold and the copper for me!" Then would all the people there separate them for you? Would anyone do so?

Questioner: Only the goldsmith would do so.

Dadashri: The one whose occupation pertains to this, the one who is an expert in this, that person would separate the gold and the copper; he would separate one hundred percent of the gold. This is because he knows the *gunadharma* (intrinsic properties with a specific function) of both, he knows that, 'Gold has these *gunadharma* and copper has these *gunadharma*.' Similarly, the *Gnani Purush* Knows the *gunadharma* of the Self and of the non-Self.

The gold and copper in this ring are in the form of a mixture, so it is possible to separate them. If gold and copper were to become a compound, then it would not be possible to separate them. Otherwise, the properties would end up becoming completely different. Similarly, the

Self and the non-Self are a mixture, and they are not in a compound form. This is why it is possible to identify their inherent nature once again. Had they become a compound, the individual inherent nature would never be found again. The *gunadharma* of the Self would not be found, nor would the *gunadharma* of the non-Self be found, and a third, entirely new *gunadharma* would emerge. However, this is not the case. This is simply a mixture that has formed. That is why when the *Gnani Purush* separates the two, the Self is realized.

What Is the Gnan Vidhi?

Questioner: What is this *Gnan Vidhi* of Yours?

Dadashri: The *Gnan Vidhi* separates the non-Self complex (*pudgal*) and the Self (*Atma*)! It separates the pure Self (*shuddha Chetan*) and the non-Self complex.

Questioner: This is fine in theory, but I want to know about the process.

Dadashri: One does not have to give anything, one simply has to sit here and repeat exactly what is being spoken. [It is a two-hour experiment of Knowledge that leads to the realization of 'who am I'. For 48 minutes, one is asked to repeat sentences of the Science of separation (*bhed Vignan*), which separates the Self and the non-Self. All those who are present are to repeat these together. Subsequently, over the course of an hour, the five *Agnas* (special directives given by the *Gnani Purush* that sustain the enlightened state after *Gnan Vidhi*) are explained in detail with examples, in which one is informed on how to conduct life from this point forward so that new karma do not get charged, how karma bound in the past can be exhausted completely, and along with that, how the established awareness (*laksh*) of 'I am pure Soul' can always prevail.]

Is a Guru or a Gnani Needed?

Questioner: What should one do if he already has a guru prior to meeting Dada?

Dadashri: If you do not wish to visit him, then it is not mandatory for you to visit him. You may go if you wish to, and if you do not wish to, then don't go. In fact, you should go simply for the reason that he does not feel hurt. You should maintain humility towards him. At the time of taking *Gnan*, if someone were to ask me, "Should I leave my guru now?" Then I would tell him, "Hey, don't leave him. It is on account of this guru that you have reached this far." By following a guru, a person remains within some boundaries. If there is no guru, then there are no boundaries either. However, you can tell your guru, "I have met a *Gnani Purush*. I go to do His *darshan* (devotional viewing)." Some people even bring their guru to 'us'. This is because the guru also wants to attain liberation, doesn't he! Knowledge of worldly life cannot be acquired without a guru, nor can the Knowledge that leads to liberation. A worldly guru is for worldly interaction (*vyavahaar*), whereas the *Gnani Purush* is for the Self and Its realm (*Nishchay*). Worldly interaction is relative, whereas the Self and Its realm is Real. A guru is needed for the relative, whereas a *Gnani Purush* is needed for the Real.

[7] What Is the Nature of Liberation?

The Only Goal Worth Having

Questioner: What goal should a person have?

Dadashri: Only that of attaining liberation (*moksha*); that should be the only goal. You too want liberation, don't you? For how much longer do you want to keep on wandering aimlessly? You have done only this for infinite lives. There is no place left where you haven't wandered, is there! You've wandered in the animal life-form, in the human life-form, in the celestial life-form; you've done nothing but wander in all of these realms of existence. Why did you have to wander? It is because you have not Known [the answer to] 'who am I'. You have not Known Your own Real form as the Self (*Swaroop*). You should Know Your Real form as the Self. Should you not Know who You are? Despite wandering so extensively, you still don't Know [the answer to] this? Is making money the only goal in life? Should you not also do a certain extent for the purpose of attaining liberation?

Questioner: It should be done.

Dadashri: So there is a need to become independent, isn't there? How long can you be dependent on things other than the Self?

Questioner: I believe it is not necessary to become independent, but it is necessary to have the understanding to become independent.

Dadashri: Yes, that understanding is necessary. If you get that understanding, then it is more than enough. It is okay if you cannot become independent; to become independent or not will come later. But even then, the understanding is necessary, isn't it? If it first comes into understanding, it is more than enough.

No Effort Is Required to Come Into the Inherent Nature as the Self

Liberation means to come into One's own inherent nature as the Self, whereas worldly life means assumed identification with that which is not one's own. So which one is easier? To remain in the inherent nature as the Self. So then, it is not difficult to attain liberation. It is always worldly life that is difficult. In comparison, liberation is even easier than preparing *khichadee* (a simple rice and lentil meal). To make *khichadee*, logs need to be sought out, rice and lentils need to be sought out, a pan needs to be sought out, water needs to be sought out; it is only after this is done that *khichadee* can be made. Whereas liberation is even easier than making *khichadee*. However, the bestower of liberation, a *Gnani*, must be found. Otherwise, liberation will never be attained; ten million years may pass by, yet it will not be attained. Have you not gone through infinite lives?

Liberation Cannot Be Attained Through Hard Work

Don't 'we' say, "Come and get your liberation from 'us'!" Yet people think, 'Of what use is liberation that is given to us without any hard work on our part!' Very well then, go ahead and attain it through hard work. Just look how splendid his understanding is! Besides, nothing will be attained through hard work. No one has ever attained liberation by putting in hard work.

Questioner: Is it possible to give or take away liberation?

Dadashri: It is not something that can be given or taken away. It is passed on through an active evidence. The fact that you have met 'us', that itself an active evidence (*nimit*). An active evidence is required. Otherwise, there is neither a giver nor is there any taker. Who is considered a giver? Someone who gives away something that belongs to him is considered a giver. In this case, liberation lies within you; 'we' simply need to show you and make you realize that. So there is no giving or taking, there is only an active evidence.

Liberation Means Eternal Bliss

Questioner: What is the point of attaining liberation?

Dadashri: When some people meet 'us', they tell 'us', "I do not want liberation." So I say to them, "Dear fellow, you may have no need for liberation, but do you want happiness or not? Or do you like misery?" To which they respond, "No, we do want happiness." So I ask, "Will it do if you have happiness to a lesser extent?" They reply, "No, we want complete happiness." So I tell them, "Then let's talk only about happiness! Forget about liberation." People do not understand what liberation really is. They merely use the word, that's all. People believe that there is a particular location that is called *moksha*, and upon going there, they will enjoy liberation! However, it is not like that.

The Two Stages of Liberation

Questioner: The conventional definition of *moksha* is freedom from the cycle of birth and death.

Dadashri: Yes, that is true. However, that is the final stage of liberation; it is the secondary stage. In the first stage, the first *moksha* refers to that in which an absence of [suffering amidst] the miseries of worldly life prevails. Even amidst the miseries of worldly life, One remains unaffected by the miseries, a blissful state (*samadhi*) prevails amidst externally-induced problems (*upadhi*); that is the first *moksha*. And then, once One leaves the physical body [permanently], ultimate liberation takes place. However, the first *moksha* should take place here and now. *Moksha* has certainly happened for 'us', hasn't it! In spite of living in worldly life, One should remain unaffected by worldly life; *moksha* of that sort should take place. It is possible for this to happen through *Akram Vignan* (the step-less Science of Self-realization).

Freedom Experienced Whilst Living

Questioner: Now in terms of this freedom (*mukti*) or liberation (*moksha*), is it freedom that is experienced while one is living or is it freedom that comes after death?

Dadashri: Of what use is freedom after you are dead? People say that you will attain freedom after you die, and upon saying so, they entrap you. Hey, show me something over here! Let me experience the taste of it, show me some proof. How can one be sure that he will attain liberation over there [after death]? Of what use is liberation that is taken 'on credit'? Nothing will be gained through liberation that is taken 'on credit'. It is better to have 'cash on hand'. You should be able to experience freedom here whilst living a worldly life, just as King Janak [an enlightened king of India who lived in 5000 BCE and who carried out all his royal duties whilst prevailing as the Self] had experienced freedom. Have you heard of this or not?

Questioner: I have heard of it.

[8] What Is the Akram Path?

Extraordinary Spiritual Powers Through Akram Gnan

Questioner: Well, is it possible to attain Self-realization so easily whilst living a worldly life?

Dadashri: Yes, there is such a way. It is possible to attain Self-realization not only whilst living a worldly life, but you can attain Self-realization even if you are living with your wife. Self-realization can be attained not only whilst living a worldly life, but you can get your children married as well as fulfill all the worldly responsibilities. I too live a worldly life and make you attain Self-realization.

Living a worldly life means, I give you all the freedom; you can go out and watch a movie, get your son married, get your daughter married, and moreover, wear beautiful clothes when you get them married. Do you need any other 'guarantee' [assurance] beyond this?

Questioner: If all such freedom is given, then one can definitely prevail in it.

Dadashri: All the freedom! This is an exceptional path. You do not have to do any hard work. 'We' will give you your own Self in your hands, so thereafter, dwell in the Self and stay in the 'lift'. 'You' do not have to do anything else. Then You will not bind any karma at all. You will bind karma only for one additional life, and that too, only to the extent You follow 'our' *Agnas* (special directives given by the *Gnani Purush* that sustain the enlightened state after *Gnan Vidhi*). The reason You should remain in 'our' *Agnas* is because you will otherwise be in trouble if you stick your hand outside the 'lift'!

Questioner: So that means there will be one more birth to take?

Dadashri: You had a past birth and you will have a future birth too. This *Gnan* is such that one or two births still remain to be taken. First comes liberation from ignorance of the Self. Then, after one or two more lifetimes, the final liberation is attained. The current era of the time cycle is such that one more birth still remains.

So, come to 'us' one day. Come on the day that 'we' decide [to have the *Gnan Vidhi*]. On that day, 'we' cut the 'rope' for everyone. 'We' do not cut it daily. Otherwise, 'we' would have to get a new blade. On ordinary days, there is *satsang* (spiritual gathering conducted in a question and answer format). But on that day which has been decided upon, 'we' directly sever the 'knot' of the 'rope'. Nothing else. Then You immediately realize that all of this has been released. Once someone who is tied up experiences being released, he will immediately say, "I have become free." Thus, the realization of having become free should take place. To become free is not a falsehood. Thus, 'we' free You.

What happens on the day 'we' give a person this *Gnan*? The person's [demerit] karma get annihilated completely in the fire of Knowledge. Two types of karma get annihilated, and one type of karma remains. The karma that are in the form of vapor get destroyed, and the karma that are in the form of water also get destroyed. And the karma that are in the form of ice do not get destroyed. This is because these karma have solidified, they are ready to give result, so then they do not let up. However, the fire of Knowledge annihilates the karma that are in the form of water and vapor. That is why people feel so light immediately upon receiving *Gnan*; the awakened awareness (*jagruti*) immediately increases for them. This is because, as long as the karma do not get annihilated, the awakened awareness would not increase for a person! The karma that are in the form of ice remain to be suffered. Nonetheless, 'we' have shown all the ways by which they become easier to suffer, such as, singing '*Dada Bhagwan Na Aseem Jai Jaikar Ho* (infinite glorious salutations to Dada Bhagwan),' saying the *Trimantra* (the three mantras that destroy all obstacles in life), and saying the Nine *Kalams* (nine statements in which one asks for energy to the pure Soul within for the highest spiritual intents).

When 'we' give *Gnan* (Knowledge of the Self), your karma get completely annihilated, and at that time, many veils of ignorance over the Self (*avaran*) break. At that time, through the grace of the Lord, One becomes aware [as the

Self]. Upon awakening as the Self, that awakened awareness (*jagruti*) does not leave. Subsequently, it is possible to remain ever aware. Thus, the conviction (*pratiti*) of 'I am pure Soul' definitely remains uninterruptedly. When does conviction prevail? If there is awakened awareness, then conviction remains. First comes the awakened awareness, then there is conviction. So, the experience (*anubhav*), established awareness (*laksh*), and conviction (*pratiti*) as the Self; these three remain. The conviction remains all the time. The established awareness remains sometimes. When we become involved in some work, we may miss out on the established awareness, and once there is respite from work, the established awareness returns. And the experience as the Self comes about when one is relieved from work and all other duties and sits in solitude; that is when the experience will be felt. Mind you, the experience will inevitably keep growing. This is because, it can be understood what Chandubhai was like before and what he is like today. So why is there this difference? It is because of the experience of the Self. Before, there was the experience of 'I am this body', whereas now, there is the experience as the Self.

Questioner: What happens when the Self has come into experience?

Dadashri: When the Self has come into experience, the belief that 'I am the body' (*dehadhyaas*) departs. When this belief departs, the binding of new karma ceases. A state that is free from the inflow of new karma (*samvar*) prevails. So what more could a person want?

The Line of Demarcation Between the Self and the Non-Self

This is *Akram Vignan*, that is why *samkit* (the right belief of 'I am pure Soul') is attained in such a short time.

Conversely, it is currently not possible for *samkit* to arise on the *Kramik* path. This *Akram Vignan* is actually a very elevated type of Science. 'We' create a division between the Self and the non-Self, meaning a division between what is Yours and what is not Yours. 'We' create a line of demarcation which defines which division is Yours and which division is not Yours. Thereafter, we should not eat the vegetables from the neighbor's farm, should we!

The Kramik Path and the Akram Path

The *Gnan* of the *Tirthankars* (the absolutely enlightened Lords who can liberate others) is *Kramik Gnan* (Knowledge obtained through the traditional step-by-step path to attain the Self). *Kramik* means to climb one step after another. As one decreases his *parigrah* (acquisitiveness towards worldly possessions), he progresses towards liberation. This may take innumerable lifetimes. And what is this *Akram Vignan*? There is no need to climb steps. One simply has to get on the 'lift' ['elevator'] and go to the twelfth floor. This is a 'lift' path of a kind that has emerged. So whoever enters the 'lift' attains salvation. 'We' are simply an active evidence (*nimit*). Whoever enters this 'lift' attains the ultimate solution! The ultimate solution will need to be brought about, won't it? Shouldn't you have the assurance that you are indeed going to attain liberation after entering the 'lift'? The assurance of that is that anger, pride, deceit, and greed do not arise, *aartadhyan* (adverse internal state that results in hurting the self) or *raudradhyan* (adverse internal state that results in hurting the self and others) do not arise. So the [spiritual] work is completed in its entirety, isn't it?

The One Who Meets 'Us' Is Qualified

Questioner: This path is so simplified, so then do we not need to have any qualifications? Is it open to anyone?

Dadashri: Some people ask 'us', "Am I qualified [to receive this *Gnan*]?" I tell them, "You have met 'us', so you are qualified." The fact that we met means there are scientific circumstantial evidences behind it. Therefore, whosoever meets 'us' is considered to be qualified. Those who do not meet 'us' are not qualified. What is the reason behind a person meeting 'us'? It is because one is qualified that he meets 'us'. Despite having met 'us', if one does not attain [Self-realization], then it is his obstructing karma that is hindering him.

On the Kramik Path, One Has to Do, and in Akram...

A man once asked, "What is the difference between the *Kramik* and the *Akram* path?" I replied, "On the *Kramik* path, everyone says to forgo bad deeds and to do good deeds. Everyone says the very same thing, that is the *Kramik* path. *Kramik* means they all tell you to forgo things, to forgo deceit and greed, and to turn towards doing good things. Is that not what you have done up until now?

Whereas this *Akram* means there is nothing that needs to be 'done'. There is no such thing as, 'I am doing' (*karomi*), 'You are doing' (*karosi*), and 'They are doing' (*karoti*)! In *Akram*, if one's pocket gets picked, then one will say, "'He' [the other person's Soul] has not picked the pocket, and 'my' [the Soul's] pocket has not been picked," whereas on the *Kramik* path, one will say, "He picked the pocket, and my pocket was picked."

Akram Vignan is like a lottery. What effort does one have to put in for the prize he receives through a lottery? He spent a rupee and other people also spent a rupee [to buy the lottery ticket], but he got lucky. Similarly, this *Akram Vignan* bestows liberation immediately, instantly!

Groundbreaking Changes Through Akram

Akram Vignan is a spectacular wonder. After attaining this *Gnan*, a person feels a significant change the very next day. Simply upon hearing this, people become convinced and are attracted to this path.

May the Akram Path Spread Worldwide

This circumstance is of a great kind, something like this has never happened anywhere. Only one person, only Dada, could accomplish this. No one else would be able to.

Questioner: And after that, Dada's grace will be at work, won't it?

Dadashri: It will continue. It is my wish that someone gets prepared for this; someone will be needed to continue this path, won't they?

Questioner: Yes, there is a need!

Dadashri: But my desire will be fulfilled.

Questioner: If this *Akram Vignan* is to continue, it will continue through a *nimit* (an apparent doer who is instrumental in a process)!

Dadashri: *Akram Vignan* itself will continue. If things continue the way they are for a year or two, then the entire world will only be talking about *Akram Vignan* and it will spread far and wide. The way false tales become the talk of the town, the right information will also become the talk of the town. The right information takes more time to be put into practice, whereas false information gets put into practice immediately.

Through Akram, There Is Moksha for Females Too

People say, "Only a male can attain liberation, females

cannot attain liberation." But I tell them, "Females can also attain liberation, why can't they?" To which they reply, "Their tubers of deceit (*kapat*) and illusory attachment (*moha*) are very big. If a male has a tuber this small, then that of a female is as large as a yam!"

Females will also attain liberation. So what if everyone says that she cannot, but females are worthy of liberation. This is because she is the Self and has come in touch [become familiarized] with the male [*prakruti*; inherent characteristic traits of the relative self]; so she will also acquire a way out. However, as the illusory attachment of the female *prakruti* is very strong, it will take more time!

Get Your Spiritual Work Done

Get your spiritual work done here, whenever you need to. It is not that you are forced to come here. Come here if you feel like coming! And if you enjoy worldly life, if you can bear it, then continue with that 'business'. From 'our' side, it isn't that you must do this or that. Nor will 'we' write a letter to you [to invite you to come]. If you happen to come here, 'we' will tell you, "Dear fellow, take advantage of this [*Gnan*]." That's all 'we' would say. Such a Science has not manifested since thousands of years. That is why 'we' are saying, "Whatever is going to happen later on, so be it, but it is worth getting your spiritual work done."

[9] Who Is the Gnani Purush?

A Sant Purush and the Gnani Purush

Questioner: What is the difference between all of these saints (*sant*) and the *Gnani Purush*?

Dadashri: Who is considered to be a saint? A saint

is someone who teaches others to forgo their weaknesses and take up good things; they teach others to stop doing bad deeds and start doing good deeds.

Questioner: So is the one who rescues us from binding demerit karma a saint?

Dadashri: Yes, the one who rescues people from binding demerit karma is a saint. However, the One who rescues people from both demerit karma and merit karma is called a *Gnani Purush*.

A saint leads people to the right path, whereas the *Gnani Purush* liberates people. The saints are following a path. They are following a path and they will tell others following a path, "Come and join me." Whereas the *Gnani Purush* is considered the final station; He will help you get your spiritual work done.

Who is a true saint? One who has no 'my-ness' (*mamata*). Others have 'my-ness' of varying degrees. And who is a true *Gnani*? The One who has neither ego (*ahamkaar*) nor 'my-ness'.

Therefore, saints are not the same as the *Gnani Purush*. Saints do not have awareness of the Self. It is when those saints meet the *Gnani Purush* that they will attain the ultimate solution. This is needed even for saints. Everyone has to come here, there is no choice, is there! Everyone has this desire.

The *Gnani Purush* is considered to be a wonder of the world. The *Gnani Purush* is considered to be a lit lamp.

Recognizing the Gnani Purush

Questioner: How can the *Gnani Purush* be recognized?

Dadashri: How can one recognize Him? The *Gnani*

Purush is such that He can be easily recognized. 'His' fragrance is identifiable. The environment around Him is entirely unique! 'His' speech is entirely unique! 'He' can be identified through His words. Oh, He can be identified simply by taking a look into His eyes. Putting everything else aside, the *Gnani Purush* gives a lot of assurance, tremendous assurance! And each and every word of His is in the form of scriptures, provided they are understood. 'His' speech, actions, and humility win over people's minds, they are such that they captivate the mind. So, He has numerous characteristics.

The *Gnani Purush* does not have even a drop of intellect. 'He' is beyond the intellect (*abudha*). Now, how many people are there who do not have even a drop of intellect? It is very rare for such a person to be born, and when that is the case, people attain salvation. Through Him, hundreds of thousands of people can swim across the ocean of worldly life and attain liberation. The *Gnani Purush* is devoid of the ego; He does not have even the slightest ego. No one in this world is devoid of the ego. The *Gnani Purush* alone is devoid of the ego.

A *Gnani Purush* manifests once across the span of thousands of years, whereas, there is an abundance of saints and experts of the scriptures. There are very many *gnanis* of the scriptures (those who have knowledge of the scriptures) over here [in India], but there are no *Gnanis* of the Self (*Atma Gnani*). The One who Knows the Self is absolutely blissful and does not have any misery, even in the slightest extent. That is why your salvation can happen through Him. The One who has attained His own salvation can bring about your salvation. The One who has crossed [the 'ocean' of worldly life] can help you get across. Otherwise, if he himself is struggling to stay afloat, then he can never help others get across.

[10] Who Is Dada Bhagwan?

Dada Bhagwan and 'I' Are Not One and the Same

Questioner: So why do you allow yourself to be addressed as God (*Bhagwan*)?

Dadashri: 'We' are not God. 'We' actually bow down to God, to Dada Bhagwan. The one who is visible here is not Dada Bhagwan. 'We' are at three hundred and fifty-six degrees [of spiritual development], whereas Dada Bhagwan is at three hundred and sixty degrees. 'We' lack four degrees, that is why 'we' too bow down to Dada Bhagwan.

Questioner: Why do you do that?

Dadashri: It is because 'we' want to complete the remaining four degrees. 'We' will have to complete them, won't 'we'? 'We' lack four degrees, 'we' failed, but do 'we' have any other choice but to pass the second time around?

Questioner: Do you have a desire to become God?

Dadashri: 'We' actually find it very burdensome to become God. 'We' are the humblest (*laghutam*) person. There is no one in this world who is humbler than me, 'we' are the humblest person. Therefore, 'we' find it burdensome to become God; on the contrary, 'we' feel bashful about it!

Questioner: If you do not want to become God, then why do you want to put in the effort to complete the four degrees?

Dadashri: It is so that 'we' attain liberation. What would 'we' gain by becoming God? Anyone who possesses Godlike attributes, any such person can become God. God is an adjective. Whoever possesses such qualities, people will unquestionably refer to him as God.

The Lord of the Fourteen Worlds Has Manifested Here

Questioner: For whom are the words 'Dada Bhagwan' used?

Dadashri: They are used for Dada Bhagwan, not for me, 'we' are actually a *Gnani Purush*.

Questioner: Which *Bhagwan*?

Dadashri: Dada Bhagwan, the One who is the Lord of the fourteen worlds. 'He' resides within you too, but He has not yet manifested within you. 'He' remains in an unexpressed form within you, whereas He has manifested within me. The One who has manifested is such that He can give you results. You will benefit even by saying His name just once. However, if you say His name with the right understanding, then you will attain salvation, and if you have any worldly difficulties, then even those will clear away. However, you should not become greedy as far as this is concerned. And if you do become greedy, then there will be no end to it. Do you understand who Dada Bhagwan is?

The one who is visible here is not Dada Bhagwan. You must be thinking that the person in front of you is Dada Bhagwan, isn't it? However, who you see here is a Patel from Bhadran [a town in Gujarat, India]; 'we' are a *Gnani Purush*, and the Lord who has manifested within is Dada Bhagwan. The Lord of the fourteen worlds has manifested; 'we' have personally Seen Him, 'we' have experienced Him. That is why 'we' are saying with a guarantee that He has manifested within.

And who is it that is speaking right now? It is a 'taped record' that is speaking. This is because Dada Bhagwan does not have the power to speak, and this Patel is speaking on the basis of the 'taped record'. This is because 'God' and 'Patel' have been separated, therefore, in that situation, egoism cannot be expressed. The 'taped record' is speaking and 'we' remain the Knower-Seer of it. Even for you, the 'taped record' is speaking, but in your mind, there is indulgence in the pleasure that arises from the doership of speaking. However, 'we' too have to bow down to Dada Bhagwan. Dada Bhagwan and 'we' are indeed separate. Whereas people think that 'we' are Dada Bhagwan. No, how could 'we' be Dada Bhagwan? This is actually a Patel from Bhadran.

[11] The Akram Path Continues

A Lineage of Gnanis Will Follow

'We' will leave behind a lineage of *Gnanis*, 'we' will set in place 'our' heirs, and subsequently, the link of *Gnanis* will continue. Therefore, seek out the living *Gnani* (*sajeevan murti*). It is not possible to arrive at the ultimate solution without Him.

'We' are personally going to give 'our' spiritual powers (*siddhis*) to some people. Won't this be necessary after 'our' departure? The future generations will need this path, won't they?

The One Whom the World Accepts Will Become the Next One

Questioner: You say, "There will be forty to fifty thousand who will mourn after me, but there will not be a single disciple." So what do you mean by this?

Dadashri: I will not have any disciples. This is not a seat of power. If it were a seat of power, then there would be an heir to it, wouldn't there! You would have to be born as a relative to become an heir, wouldn't you! Here, the

One who will be accepted will become the next one. The One who becomes everyone's disciple will be the suitable One. In this case, the One whom the world accepts will become the next One. The world will accept the One who becomes the humblest of all!

[12] After Attaining the Vision as the Self...

The Signs of Having Attained Self-Realization

Before receiving *Gnan*, you were Chandubhai and currently, after attaining *Gnan*, You have become the pure Soul. Is there any difference in Your experience?

Questioner: Yes.

Dadashri: How long does the experiential awareness (*bhaan*) of 'I am pure Soul' remain for You?

Questioner: When I am sitting alone in a solitary place.

Dadashri: Yes. After that, what belief (*bhaav*) prevails? Do You ever have the belief that 'I am Chandubhai'? Have You ever really had the belief that 'I am Chandubhai' [after attaining *Gnan*]?

Questioner: It has not happened after taking *Gnan*.

Dadashri: So then You are indeed the pure Soul. A person has only one belief. So 'I am pure Soul' indeed remains for You constantly.

Questioner: But many times in worldly interaction, the experiential awareness of the pure Soul does not remain.

Dadashri: Then does the internal state of 'I am Chandubhai' remain? Suppose for three hours, the internal state of the pure Soul does not remain, and after three hours

You are asked, "Are You Chandubhai or the pure Soul?" Then what would You say?

Questioner: The pure Soul.

Dadashri: This means that the internal state [of awareness as the Self] was certainly there. Suppose there is a businessman who is drunk; at that time, he loses his internal state [of awareness]. But what happens once the effect of the alcohol wears off?

Questioner: He becomes aware once again.

Dadashri: Similarly, this is how the other external effects are.

If I ask You, "Are You really Chandubhai or are You the pure Soul?" Then You reply, "The pure Soul." If I ask You the next day, "Who are You really?" Then You reply, "The pure Soul." After asking You the same for five days, 'we' would understand that your master key is with 'us'. Then even if you protest, 'we' would not listen to you. 'We' would let you go on protesting.

The Emergence of Unprecedented Awareness

What has Shrimad Rajchandra [Self-realized *Gnani Purush* who lived between 1867-1901] said about this? "*Sadguruna updeshthi aavyu apoorva bhaan, nijpad nijmahi lahyu, door thayu agnan.*" (Through the teachings of a Self-realized spiritual teacher, unprecedented awareness has emerged. The state of 'I' has become established in the Self, the ignorance of the Self has departed.) Earlier, there was only the awareness of 'I am the body.' Earlier, we did not have any awareness beyond that of 'I am the body.' So now, the unprecedented awareness, the experiential awareness (*bhaan*) of the Self has emerged for 'us'. The state the 'I' was in before, the 'I' used to say,

"I am Chandubhai"; now that 'I' has become established in the Self. The state the 'I' was in before, it has now become established in the Self. And the ignorance that was there, [the belief] of 'I am Chandubhai,' that ignorance has departed.

That Is Considered the Belief That 'I am the Body'

All the people in this world are not able to let go of the belief that 'I am the body' and they are not able to remain in their own Real form as the Self. The fact that You have remained in the Self means the egoism is gone, the 'my-ness' has departed. 'I am Chandubhai' is considered *dehadhyaas* (the belief that 'I am the body'), and from the point the established awareness (*laksh*) of 'I am pure Soul' sets in, no *adhyaas* (the ingrained belief of 'I am Chandubhai' that has come into conduct) remains whatsoever. None of that remains anymore. Even then, if any mistake happens, only slight suffocation arises.

The State of the Pure Soul Is Indeed Pure

So after attaining this *Gnan*, the illusion that was previously there of 'I am doing,' that awareness has shattered. Thus, 'we' have referred to It [the 'I'] as the pure Soul so that the experiential awareness that 'I am indeed pure' remains. No matter what happens with anyone, even if Chandubhai hurls abuses at someone, You are still pure. So then, You should tell Chandubhai, 'Why are you hurting the other person? Now do *pratikraman* (confess, apologize and resolve not to repeat a mistake).'

When you say something that hurts someone, that is considered as having done *atikraman* (to hurt any other living being through the mind, speech, or body). In such a case, *pratikraman* should be done for it.

Pratikraman means to ask for forgiveness in whatever

way you understand how to. 'I understand that this is a fault of mine, and I will not repeat this fault again'; you should decide on this. You should make a pledge, 'What I have done is wrong, this should not be done. I will not do this again.' Yet if it happens again and the same fault is repeated, then you should repent over it again. But for however much you identify, as you repent over it, it decreases by that much. In this way, it will gradually come to an end.

Questioner: So how should we do *pratikraman* for any person?

Dadashri: First recall the pure Soul, who is completely separate from the mind, body, and speech, charge karma, subtle discharge karma, and gross discharge karma, [the name of the person] and all illusion related to [the name of the person]. And then recall the mistakes that were made [*alochana*]. [Say internally,] 'I repent over these mistakes, please forgive me for these mistakes [*pratikraman*]. I am making the firm resolve to not repeat these mistakes [*pratyakhyan*].' 'You' should remain the Knower-Seer of Chandubhai and Know how many *pratikraman* Chandubhai does, how well he does them, and how many times he does them.

Pragnya Cautions You From Within

This is a Science, so You will experience It, and It will caution You from within. In the other case [in the traditional step-by-step path of spiritual progress], you have to set out to do things, whereas This cautions You from within.

Questioner: Now 'I' have gotten the experience that the cautioning takes place from within.

Dadashri: 'You' have now found this path and have

entered the first 'door' within the boundary of the pure Soul. No one can turn You back from here. No one has the authority to turn You back; You have entered such a place!

Who keeps cautioning You again and again? *Pragnya* (the liberating energy of the Self) does! *Pragnya* does not emerge until one attains *Gnan*. In other words, *Pragnya* begins upon attaining the right belief of 'I am pure Soul.' How does *Pragnya* begin when the right belief of 'I am pure Soul' is attained? It is like the second day of the lunar cycle. For us [*mahatmas*] over here, *Pragnya* is fully expressed. It is *Pragnya* that is fully expressed, so then It cautions You only for the purpose of taking You to liberation. King Bharat [who had attained *Akram Gnan* from his father, the fully enlightened *Tirthankar* Lord Rushabhdev] had to employ people to caution him; he had servants who would call out every fifteen minutes and say three times, "King Bharat, take heed, take heed, take heed." Look, for You, *Pragnya* cautions You from within. *Pragnya* keeps cautioning You, 'Hey, don't do that.' 'It' keeps cautioning You all day long. And that Itself is the experience of the Self! There is the constant experience of the Self all day long.

The Experience Undoubtedly Lies Within

On the night 'we' give you *Gnan*, the experience which takes place on that night never leaves. How could it possibly ever leave! On the day 'we' gave you *Gnan*, the experience that takes place that night remains forever. However, later on, your karma take over, the karma that had been charged in the past life, the suffering that remains pending, those 'creditors' come to recover their debt; what can 'we' possibly do in that?

Questioner: But Dada, the same extent of suffering is not felt anymore.

Dadashri: No. The fact that it is not felt to the same extent is a different matter. However, for the one who has more 'creditors', he gets ambushed to a greater extent. If there are five 'creditors', then he will get ambushed by five of them, if there are two, then he will get ambushed by two, and if there are twenty, then then he will get ambushed by twenty. 'We' have placed You in the state of the pure Soul, but when the force of karma comes the next day, you feel a bit of suffocation.

What Remains Pending Now?

That other is the science of the *Kramik* path and this is *Akram Vignan*. This Knowledge is verily of the absolutely detached (*vitaraag*) Lords. There is no difference in the Knowledge. After 'we' give *Gnan*, You experience the Self, so what is left for You to 'do'? To follow the *Agnas* of the *Gnani Purush*. The *Agnas* themselves are the religion and the *Agnas* themselves are the penance. And 'our' *Agnas* are never restrictive towards worldly life in any way. Despite living in worldly life, nothing of worldly life will affect You. This is what *Akram Vignan* is like.

So if You want to attain the state whereby You can attain final liberation after just one more life (*ekavatari*), then follow the *Agnas* as per what 'we' tell You. Then this Science is such that You will attain final liberation after just one more life. Although this Science is there, it is still not possible to attain liberation directly from here [*Bharat Kshetra*; the location in the universe where planet Earth exists, and in which it is currently the fifth era of the time cycle, during which final liberation is not possible].

On the Path of Liberation, the Agnas Themselves are the Religion

The one who wants to attain liberation does not need rituals. The one who wants to attain a life-form in the celestial realm, the one who wants worldly pleasures, needs to carry out rituals. The one who wants to attain liberation needs only the Knowledge of the Self (*Gnan*) and the *Agnas* of the *Gnani*.

There is no need for any penance (*tapa*) or renunciation (*tyaag*) on the path of liberation. If one simply meets the *Gnani Purush*, then the *Agnas* of the *Gnani* are themselves the religion, and the *Agnas* are themselves the penance. And they are indeed the Knowledge (*Gnan*), Vision (*Darshan*), Conduct (*Charitra*), Penance (*Tapa*); the direct result of which is *moksha*.

Stay Put Close to the Gnani

Feelings of love have never arisen for the *Gnani*. And once feelings of love arise for the *Gnani*, all of the solutions will follow. In every lifetime, there has been nothing else except [devotion towards] a wife and children!

The Lord had said that after attaining the right belief of 'I am pure Soul' (*samkit*) from the *Gnani Purush*, pursue the *Gnani Purush*.

Questioner: In what sense should we pursue Him?

Dadashri: In the sense that, after attaining this *Gnan*, there should be no other devotion. However, 'we' know that this is *Akram*. These people have come with countless 'files' [Dadashri's special term for karmic accounts that take one away from the Self and into worldly life]. Therefore, 'we' have given You the liberty to go and clear these 'files'. But this does not mean that Your [spiritual] work is done. These days, there are a great many 'files', so if 'we' were to keep You with 'us', your 'files' would come here to call You back. That is why 'we' have given You the freedom to go home and settle the 'files' with equanimity. Otherwise, One should exclusively stay put close to the *Gnani*.

This aside, it should bother You constantly, day and night, that You are not able to fully benefit. 'You' may have 'files'; the *Gnani Purush* has said, He has made it an *Agna* to clear the 'files' with equanimity. So the *Agnas* themselves are the religion (*dharma*), aren't they? That is our *dharma*. However, You should keep feeling regret that, 'May these files decrease so that I can take benefit.'

For Him, Mahavideh Kshetra Will Come Readily

And the One for whom the established awareness (*laksh*) of the pure Soul has set in over here, such a person cannot remain here in *Bharat Kshetra*. It is a natural law that the One for whom the established awareness of the Self has set in, such a person certainly reaches *Mahavideh Kshetra* (one of the three locations in the universe where human beings reside. Living *Tirthankar* Lords always exist in *Mahavideh Kshetra*, so it is always possible for living beings to attain final liberation from there)! Such a person would not be able to remain here, in this *Dushamkaal* (the current era of the time cycle, characterized by a lack of unity in thought, speech, and action). Once the established awareness of the pure Soul has set in, One will spend one or two more lives, and after doing *darshan* (devotional viewing) of the *Tirthankar* Lord Simandhar Swami in *Mahavideh Kshetra*, He will attain final liberation. That is how easy and straightforward this path is! Remain in 'our' *Agnas*. The *Agnas* are the religion, and the *Agnas* are the penance! Clear [the 'files'] with equanimity. Of all the *Agnas* that have been given, remain in them as much as You can. If You remain in them completely, then it is possible to remain [in a state] similar to that of Lord Mahavir! If You go on Seeing the Real and the relative, then your *chit* (subtle component of vision and knowledge) will not go anywhere else. However, during that time, if something arises in the mind, then you get entangled.

[13] The Importance of the Five Agnas

What Spiritual Practice Needs to Be Done After Gnan?

Questioner: What type of spiritual practice (*sadhana*) should One do after attaining this *Gnan*?

Dadashri: The only spiritual practice is to follow the five *Agnas*! There is no other *sadhana* now. All other *sadhana* leads to bondage. These five *Agnas* lead to release from bondage.

The Agnas Are Such That Samadhi Prevails

Questioner: Is there anything that is higher than these five *Agnas*?

Dadashri: These five *Agnas* are a protective enclosure so that nobody can take away Your priceless treasure. If You maintain that protective enclosure, then the *Gnan* will remain exactly as 'we' have given It to You, and if the protective enclosure becomes weakened, then someone will enter in and cause havoc. So then 'we' will have to come back to repair it. So as long as You stay within the five *Agnas*, 'we' give the guarantee that there will be constant *samadhi* (a blissful state that comes about when one becomes free from mental, physical, and externally-induced suffering).

'We' are giving You the five *Agnas* for protection. 'We' have given You this *Gnan* and with the Knowledge of separation, the separation has already happened. However, in order for this separation to prevail, 'we' are giving You the five *Agnas* for protection. This is so that You do not get robbed of that [invaluable treasure of *Gnan*] by all, as it is *Kaliyug* (the current era of the time cycle, which is characterized by moral and spiritual decline). For the seed of *Gnan* to blossom, It has to be watered and nurtured, doesn't It? Does a small protective enclosure not need to be put in place?

Only the Firm Resolve Makes You Follow the Agnas

To want to follow Dada's *Agnas* is the greatest thing of all. You should make the decision to follow the *Agnas*. Do not scrutinize whether or not You are able to follow the *Agnas*. However much You are able to follow the *Agnas* is correct. However, You should decide that You want to follow the *Agnas*.

Questioner: There is no problem if the *Agnas* are not followed completely, is there?

Dadashri: It is not that there is no problem. 'You' should decide that You definitely want to follow the *Agnas*! From the time you wake up in the morning, decide, 'I only want to stay in the five *Agnas*, I want to follow them.' From the moment You decide this, You will have come into 'our' *Agnas*, and that is all 'we' want. 'We' Know the reasons You are not able to follow them. 'You' should definitely decide, 'I want to follow them!'

[Those who have attained and follow] Our *Gnan* will definitely attain liberation. If You remain in the *Agnas*, then You will attain liberation. There are no two ways about it. And even if One is not following them, because He has attained *Gnan*, the *Gnan* will not refrain from growing. So people ask me, "Some people who have attained *Gnan* do not follow the *Agnas*, so what will happen to them? I tell them, "You do not need to be concerned about that. I need to look after that. They have taken *Gnan* from 'us', haven't they! It's not as though You have incurred a loss, is it!" This is because the demerit karma does not refrain from being annihilated. It has become hollow from within. If You remain in 'our' five *Agnas*, then You will succeed. 'We' constantly remain in the five *Agnas*, and the state 'we' prevail in, 'we' have given You that state. If You remain in the *Agnas*, then Your [spiritual] work will be done. If one tries to attain this through his own efforts for a hundred thousand lifetimes, even then he would not succeed. As it is, One follows the *Agnas* using His own judgement; He understands the *Agnas* through His own understanding, doesn't He! So there is some leakage that keeps happening. Nevertheless, the intent He has behind following the *Agnas* is that 'I want to follow the *Agnas*.' Thus, awakened awareness (*jagruti*) is required.

If You forget to follow the *Agnas*, then do *pratikraman* for it. 'You' may forget; after all, you are only human. However, do *pratikraman* for forgetting by saying, 'Oh Dada, I forgot during these two hours, I forgot Your *Agnas*. However, I do want to follow the *Agnas*. Please forgive me.' Then You will get full passing marks; You will get one hundred percent marks. So You will be relieved of Your responsibility. Once You come into the *Agnas*, nothing in the entire world will affect You. If You follow 'our' *Agnas*, then nothing will affect You. So does the responsibility fall on the One who gives the *Agnas*? No, because He is doing it for the benefit of others. So it does not affect Him and everything dissolves.

These are the Agnas of the Lord!

To follow Dada's *Agnas* does not mean that they are A. M. Patel's *Agnas*. The *Agnas* are of Dada Bhagwan Himself, the One who is the Lord of the fourteen worlds; 'We' are giving the guarantee of this. As it turns out, this discussion [about the *Agnas*] has been expressed through me. So You should follow the *Agnas*. They are not my *Agnas*, they are Dada Bhagwan's *Agnas*. 'We' [the *Gnani Purush*], too, remain in these *Agnas*, don't 'we'!

Jai Sat Chit Anand
(Awareness of the Eternal is Bliss)

Spiritual Glossary

Gujarati Word	English Translation
aaropit bhaav	false attribution of 'I am Chandubhai'
Agnas (also referred to as the five *Agnas*)	special directives given by the *Gnani Purush* that sustain the enlightened state after *Gnan Vidhi*
ahamkaar	ego
Akram	step-less
Akram Vignan	the spiritual Science of the step-less path to Self-realization
anubhav	experience as the Self
Atma	the Self; the Soul
bhaan	realization; experiential awareness
Bhagwan	God
Bharat Kshetra	the location in the universe where planet Earth exists, and in which it is currently the fifth era of the time cycle, during which final liberation is not possible
bhed Gnan	the Knowledge of separation
bhed Vignan	the Science that separates the Self from the non-Self
chit	the subtle component of vision and knowledge in the inner functioning instrument which is composed of the mind, intellect, *chit*, and ego
darshan	devotional viewing
'files'	Dadashri's special term for karmic accounts that take one away from the Self and into worldly life
Gnan	the Knowledge of the Self attained through Self-realization

Gnan Vidhi	the original scientific experiment for Self-realization which can be attained within two hours
Gnani	the One with Knowledge of the Self
Gnani Purush	the One who has realized the Self and is able to do the same for others
gunadharma	intrinsic properties with a specific function
jagruti	awakened awareness as the Self
jeevatma	embodied self
Kramik	traditional step-by-step path of spiritual progress; traditional spiritual path of penance and austerities
laksh	established awareness
mahatmas	Self-realized Ones in *Akram Vignan*
Mahavideh Kshetra	one of the three locations in the universe where human beings reside. Living *Tirthankar* Lords always exist in *Mahavideh Kshetra,* so it is always possible for living beings to attain final liberation from there.
moksha	liberation
mukti	freedom; liberation from the cycle of birth and death
nimit	active evidence; evidentiary instrument; an apparent doer who is simply instrumental in the process
Parmatma	the absolute Self
Pragnya	the liberating energy of the Self
prakruti	inherent characteristic traits of the relative self
pratikraman	to confess, apologize and resolve not to repeat a mistake

pratiti	conviction as the Self
sadhana	spiritual practice
samadhi	a blissful state that comes about when one becomes free from mental, physical and externally induced suffering
samkit	the right belief of 'I am pure Soul'
sansaar	worldly life
sant (also known as *sant purush*)	a saint
Simandhar Swami	a living *Tirthankar* Lord who resides in *Mahavideh Kshetra*. Of all the living *Tirthankar* Lords, Simandhar Swami is closest to our world and has a special connection for the salvation of the people of our world due to past karmic ties.
Swaroop	Real form as the Self
Tirthankar	the absolutely enlightened Lord who can liberate others
vyavahaar	worldly interaction

❖ ❖ ❖ ❖ ❖

Daily Prayers
Morning Prayer - Pratah Vidhi

- I bow down to Shri Simandhar Swami. (5)
- I bow down to Dada Bhagwan who is the embodiment of pure love. (5)
- May no living being in this world be hurt, even to the slightest extent, through this mind, speech or body. (5)
- With the exception of the exclusive experience of the pure Soul, I have no desire for any temporary thing of this world. (5)
- May I attain the absolute energy to remain continuously only in the Agnas of the manifest Gnani Purush, 'Dada Bhagwan'. (5)
- May the absolute Knowledge, absolute Vision, and absolute Conduct of the Science of Absolutism of Gnani Purush 'Dada Bhagwan' manifest in exactness, completely and totally. (5)

Namaskaar Vidhi
The Vidhi of Salutations

- With the live presence of 'Dada Bhagwan' as my witness, with utmost reverence and devotion, I bow to Tirthankar Lord 'Shri Simandhar Swami' who currently lives in Mahavideh Kshetra. (40)
- With the live presence of 'Dada Bhagwan' as my witness, with utmost reverence and devotion, I bow to the 'Om Parmeshthi Lords' who currently live in Mahavideh Kshetra and other Kshetra. (5)
- With the live presence of 'Dada Bhagwan' as my witness, with utmost reverence and devotion, I bow to the 'Panch Parmeshthi Lords' who currently live in Mahavideh Kshetra and other Kshetra. (5)

- With the live presence of 'Dada Bhagwan' as my witness, with utmost reverence and devotion, I bow to all the Tirthankar Lords who currently live in Mahavideh Kshetra and other Kshetra. (5)

- With utmost reverence and devotion, I bow to all the celestial beings who protect the spiritual reign of the Tirthankar Lords. (5)

- With utmost reverence and devotion, I bow to all celestial beings who protect without partiality. (5)

- With utmost reverence and devotion, I bow to the twenty-four Tirthankar Lords. (5)

- With utmost reverence and devotion, I bow to Lord Shri Krishna. (5)

- With utmost reverence and devotion as the Self, I bow to the omniscient One, Shri 'Dada Bhagwan' whose subtle presence is in our world (Bharat Kshetra). (5)

- With utmost reverence and devotion, I bow to all the 'Self-realized mahatmas' of 'Dada Bhagwan.' (5)

- With utmost reverence and devotion, I bow to the 'real Self' in all living beings of this universe. (5)

- The real Self within all living beings is divine, and therefore, I see the divine Self in all living beings. (5)

- The real Self within all beings is the pure Soul, and therefore, I see the pure Soul in all living beings in the world. (5)

- The real nature of all is eternal and elemental and with this Knowledge, I see the entire world. (5)

❖ ❖ ❖ ❖ ❖

Nav Kalamo
Nine Deep Inner Intents

1. Oh Dada Bhagwan, give me the absolute energy not to hurt, cause anyone to hurt, nor instigate anyone to hurt the ego of any living being, even to the slightest extent.

   Give me the absolute energy not to hurt, even to the slightest extent, the ego of any living being, and to conduct my thoughts, speech, and action in a manner that is accepted by all.

2. Oh Dada Bhagwan, give me the absolute energy not to hurt, cause anyone to hurt, nor instigate anyone to hurt the foundation of any religion, even to the slightest extent.

   Give me the absolute energy not to hurt, even to the slightest extent, the foundation of any religion and to conduct my thoughts, speech, and action in a manner that is accepted by all.

3. Oh Dada Bhagwan, give me the absolute energy not to criticize, offend, or disrespect any living preacher, monk, nun, or religious head.

4. Oh Dada Bhagwan, give me the absolute energy not to, nor cause anyone to, nor instigate anyone to, dislike or have contempt for any living being, even to the slightest extent.

5. Oh Dada Bhagwan, give me the absolute energy not to, nor cause anyone to, nor instigate anyone to speak any harsh or hurtful language towards any living being, even to the slightest extent.

   If someone speaks in harsh or hurtful language, give me the energy to speak kindly and softly in reply.

6. Oh Dada Bhagwan, give me the absolute energy not to have, nor cause anyone to have, nor instigate anyone to have, even to the slightest extent, any sexual faults, desires, gestures, or faults related to sexual thoughts towards any living being, be it male, female, or of bisexual orientation.

   Give me the absolute energy to be continuously free from all sexual impulses.

7. Oh Dada Bhagwan, give me the energy to not have excessive temptation towards any particular food taste.

   Give me the absolute energy to take meals with a balance of all tastes.

8. Oh Dada Bhagwan, give me the absolute energy not to, nor cause anyone to, nor instigate anyone to criticize, offend, or disrespect any being, be they present or absent, living or dead.

9. Oh Dada Bhagwan, give me the absolute energy to become an instrument for the salvation of the world.

(For further clarification, please read the book 'The Essence of All Religion' by Dadashri.)

❖ ❖ ❖ ❖ ❖

Prayer to the Pure Soul

Oh Lord within! You reside within all living beings, in the same way, You also reside within me. My real form is the same as Yours. My real form is the pure Soul.

Oh pure Soul ! With utmost devotion and oneness, I offer my salutations to You.

I confess to You all the mistakes [*recall them internally*] that I have committed in my ignorant state. I am sincerely and deeply repentant for these mistakes and ask for forgiveness. Oh Lord, please forgive me, forgive me, forgive me, and grant me the energy to never repeat such mistakes!

Oh pure Soul ! Please bless me with such grace that this feeling of separation from You terminates and that I attain oneness with You. May I remain merged in You and remain as one with You.

❖ ❖ ❖ ❖ ❖

The Vidhi for Those Who Want to Attain Self-Realization

With utmost reverence and devotion, I bow down to the manifest Gnani Purush, Dada Bhagwan.

With utmost reverence and devotion, I bow down to those Self-realized Ones who have attained the Self through the manifest Gnani Purush.

With utmost reverence and devotion, I bow down to all the celestial beings who protect without partiality.

Oh manifest Gnani Purush, Oh Self-realized Ones! Please grant salvation to this world that is currently ablaze [in misery], and with the pure intention that I become an instrument for this, I pray before You with full concentration of the mind, speech and body. May this prayer materialize to the fullest.

Oh Dada Bhagwan! The pure Knowledge-laden aphorisms, that You have Seen in Your pure Knowledge and that have been expressed in Your divine speech, are as below.

"Amidst all the worldly desires and intents of the mind, speech, and body that tend to anoint, the pure Self remains totally unanointed." (3)

"The pure Self is completely separate from all actions of the mind, speech, and body." (3)

"The pure Self knows the habits of the mind, speech, and body and the nature of those habits, and the pure Self also Knows Its own nature. This is because It [the pure Self] illuminates Itself and the non-Self." (3)

"The eater eats and the pure Self, the 'non-eater', is the Knower of this." (3)

"Gross circumstances, subtle circumstances, and the circumstances of speech are of the non-Self, and are dependent entirely on external factors, and the pure Self is only the Knower and Seer of these." (3)

"The pure Self is only the Knower-Seer of all the worldly phases, from the grossest to the subtlest, and in all of them, the pure Self is immiscible and in the form of infinite bliss." (3)

"The temporary states of the mind, speech, and body are simply natural occurrences. There is no higher authority that is their doer, and they are a result of scientific circumstantial evidence (vyavasthit)." (3)

"Not a single property of the non-Self belongs to the pure Self and not a single property of the pure Self belongs to the non-Self. The two are completely separate in every way." (3)

"All the inner intents of the transitory part are those of the non-Self. They are not of the pure Self, which is unchanging." (3)

Oh Lord! Due to illusion, I have not understood in exactness, as it should be, that the inner intents of the pure Self are precisely as mentioned in the aphorisms above. This is because upon observing myself impartially, I realize that the conflicts within me as well as outwardly expressed anger and internal turmoil have not gone. Therefore, Oh Lord! Give me the absolute energy to overcome the conflicts within me. Now, I do not yearn for anything else except to understand these pure intents of mine exactly as they are. I only yearn for liberation. For this purpose, it is my firm aspiration to only remain in the inner intent that 'I do not know anything at all,' while staying humble towards the Self-realized Ones and absolutely humble towards the Gnani Purush.

The pure intents mentioned in the above aphorisms have not come into my conviction, nor have they come into my Knowledge. If these inner intents come firmly into my conviction, only then will I experience that I have attained the true right belief of 'I am pure Soul.' For this, only two things are primarily required:

(1) Adherence to the inner intent that 'I yearn only for the absolute truth [the Self].'

(2) The absolute truth [the Self] can only be attained through complete devotion towards the Gnani Purush's Agnas.

There is no other way [to attain Self-realization] except that of meeting the living Gnani Purush. Therefore, may I remain in search of a living Gnani Purush and I am making the firm decision and resolve to remain exclusively devoted to His Agnas upon meeting Him. May this yearning of mine be fulfilled.

❖ ❖ ❖ ❖ ❖

'Dada Bhagwan Na Aseem Jai Jai Kar Ho'
'Infinite glorious salutations to Dada Bhagwan [the Lord within]'
(Say or sing aloud daily for a minimum of 10 minutes and up to 50 minutes.)

❖ ❖ ❖ ❖ ❖

Pratikraman Vidhi

Three-Step Process of Reversal from a Mistake

1. Alochana: Heart-felt inner confession of one's mistakes.

2. Pratikraman: Process of apology coupled with remorse for any wrongdoing.

3. Pratyakhyan: Sincere pledge to never repeat the mistakes.

With Dada Bhagwan as a witness, oh pure Soul of [*insert the name of the person you have hurt*]**, who is separate from the activity of the mind, speech, body, charge karma, subtle discharge karma, and gross discharge karma, with You as a witness, I am asking for forgiveness for whichever faults I have done*, up to this day. I atone for them with all my heart. Forgive me, forgive me, forgive me, and I am making the firm resolve to never repeat such faults again. Grant me the absolute energy for this.**

* Recall internally the faults in which you have hurt the other person through anger-pride-deceit-greed, sexuality, and so on.

❖ ❖ ❖ ❖ ❖

Contacts

Dada Bhagwan Foundation

India :

Adalaj (Main Center)	: **Trimandir**, Simandhar City, Ahmedabad-Kalol Highway, Adalaj, Dist.: Gandhinagar - 382421, Gujarat, India. **Tel :** + 91 79 35002100, +91 9328661166-77 **Email :** info@dadabhagwan.org
Bangalore	: +91 95909 79099
Delhi	: +91 98100 98564
Kolkata	: +91 98300 93230
Mumbai	: +91 93235 28901

Other Countries :

Argentina	: **Tel:** +54 9 376 4952565 **Email:** info@dadabhagwan.ar
Australia	: **Tel:** +61 402179706 **Email:** sydney@au.dadabhagwan.org
Brazil	: **Tel:** +55 11999828971 **Email:** info@br.dadabhagwan.org
Germany	: **Tel:** +49 700 DADASHRI (32327474) **Email:** info@dadabhagwan.de
Kenya	: **Tel:** +254 79592 DADA (3232) **Email:** info@ke.dadabhagwan.org
New Zealand	: **Tel:** +64 21 0376434 **Email:** info@nz.dadabhagwan.org
Singapore	: **Tel:** + 65 91457800 **Email:** info@sg.dadabhagwan.org
Spain	: **Tel:** +34 606245646 **Email:** info@dadabhagwan.es
UAE	: **Tel:** +971 557316937 **Email:** dubai@ae.dadabhagwan.org
UK	: **Tel :** +44 330-111-DADA (3232) **Email :** info@uk.dadabhagwan.org
USA-Canada	: **Tel :** +1 877-505-DADA (3232) **Email :** info@us.dadabhagwan.org

Website : www.dadabhagwan.org